Blood, Guts and Things that Drive You Nuts

20 Life-Changing Lessons from 20 Years on the Street

CHRIS SWANSON

Blood, Guts and Things That Drive You Nuts

20 Life-Changing Lessons from 20 Years on the Street

Copyright ©2017 by Christopher Swanson

Published by Corporate Disk Co. www.DISK.com

Printed in the United States of America
Cover photo by Gavin Smith Photography

PARENTAL ADVIVSORY

Some of the stories contained in this book are graphic and may not be suitable for certain age groups.
Parental overview and guidance is strongly suggested.

For more information about Chris Swanson, or to contact him go to:

https://www.facebook.com/SwansonLeadership
https://twitter.com/crswanson
http://instagram.com/chris_swanson262
https://www.linkedin.com/in/chris_swanson262
https://www.youtube.com/user/swansonleadership
https://swansonleadership.com

This book is dedicated to the victims who wish they could teach you from their grave, but will never have the chance. May what happened to them never be forgotten and their memories live on ...

Contents

INTRODUCTION

Livin' in the Belly of the Beast

Over the last 20 years I've dealt with crazy people, homeless people, violent people, old people, sick people, and dead people. People who love the police as well as more and more people who hate the police.

I've spent hours with serial killers, serial rapists, thieves, psychopaths, and sociopaths. I've helped protect Tiger Woods, Bill Clinton, George W. Bush, Barack Obama, Al Gore, Dick Cheney, Joe Biden, Hillary Clinton, Ted Kennedy, Bernie Sanders, Bob Dole, and Donald Trump.

I've worked through snow emergencies, deadly fires, tornadoes, floods, civil unrest, poisoned water, and human stampedes. I've stuck my hands in the bloody chests of stabbing victims. I've pulled drowned kids out of the water, sealed bloody body bags with parts in plastic, picked up fingers, and scooped up humans at every stage of decomposition. I've responded to hangings, overdoses, self-inflicted gunshot wounds, child abuses, and sexual assaults.

I've witnessed people cut in half. I've arrested both men and women for domestic violence, chased bank robbers, been sued, gone toe-to-toe with corrupt politicians, arrested dirty cops, and publicly challenged unethical lawyers, of which there are plenty.

I've delivered babies, interrogated felons, delivered turkeys on Thanksgiving, and bought crack cocaine out of the side garage door of a dope house in the projects, all while undercover.

I've told parents their children are dead and children their parents are dead. I've done more and seen more *Blood, Guts, and Things that Drive You Nuts* than I ever thought a kid with a bad haircut growing up on a ten-acre farm cleaning horse stalls on Saturday mornings should ever see.

All of this begs the question … WHY?

There are two answers:
1) **Life is about Choices or Chances.**
2) **Some things you have control of and other things just happen**.

It doesn't matter if you are a police officer, school teacher, pastor, student, plumber, pipe fitter, painter, dentist, or work at Home Depot. The question you need to ask yourself is this: How will you respond when life hits you between the eyes? What choices are you going to make?

Make no mistake, what you do will either positively or negatively impact your life *and* the world around you.

What you're about to read are 20 police stories. Some are graphic, but all are real—not embellished from someone else's playbook. This is my journey. The theme from each chapter will be followed by action steps you can implement in your life right now, today, without waiting. Don't let the fear of death or the pain of rejection be the anchor that keeps you on the bottom while driving you nuts.

This is your call to action.
It's time to work …

"Sir, What Size Shoe Is on Your Head?"

Everybody hired at the sheriff's office in Genesee County starts by working in the jail. I was 20 years old when I began my journey. Back then, we didn't have half the training I offer my staff today. In fact, there was very little formal training for new deputies. We learned most of what's needed on the job. Within one month of starting at the jail, on June 2, 1993, I was the sole deputy on a floor that housed the suicidal, the mentally insane, the injured, and the invalid. We call it Observation Housing.

At each shift change, one deputy from the shift prior gave a report of the floor's activities to the relieving deputy. As I walked in the pod for my first day on Observation Housing, the deputy I relieved reported that Inmate #11 had a "bad night," and I should expect some wild behavior.

Now a bad night under normal circumstances can be bad. But a bad night on this floor means something totally different!

I began my floor checks at the start of the shift with cell #1, checking for anything unusual or dangerous. All the way through to cells 9 and 10, there was nothing unusual to report. Then I turned the corner and looked inside the window of cell #11. There before me stood a 5' 4" naked Latino. His cell had poop smeared like wallpaper, his clothes were ripped into strips. His shoe was torn in half and on his head, making him look like Peter Pan. This, my friend, is a bad night.

As I nervously peered into his cell, thankfully sealed by safety glass, he looked at me as normal as one could with poop smeared everywhere. All I could do was smile, which he returned. It was then I realized we weren't in Kansas anymore. This was the real deal. Mentally disturbed people can be very intimidating because they are unpredictable and sometimes volatile. That's why standing in front of naked Peter Pan was so shocking to me. I'd never seen anything like that before. I also learned we appear crazy to each other every day. We are all different. Mentally ill people often believe what they are doing is totally normal and what we do is abnormal. Either way, we need to respect each other. And that's exactly what I did. I left him alone in his fantasy world until I could get hazmat and clean the "wallpaper."

There was no easing into this job. There was no sticking my foot in the water to see how cold it was. This was the real deal.

_____

Impact Theme:
As different as some people may be, accept and respect them for who they are.

Action Step:
1. No matter what you are doing, expect the unexpected.
2. Ready never comes, jump now.

3. What is abnormal for you may be someone else's normal. Be tolerant and understanding.

-2-

Chased by a Mushroom

Fresh out of the police academy, I was fortunate enough to be assigned to a drug team in the north end of Flint. It was called the Beecher Area Narcotic Group (BANG). We were a three-man team: George T, Don U, and me. We all had nicknames. I was Hollywood, Donnie was B.A. for Bad Attitude, and George was Wyatt, because he looked like Wyatt Earp with the mustache and all. (These names are used to protect their identity, except mine.) Donnie and George were veterans, and I was the rookie. Actually, I was less than a rookie. I was a rookie full of arrogance with ZERO experience. Arrogance is an attitude in police work that doesn't last long when you work with veteran cops.

I did, however, have a lot of energy and passion. When I was first assigned to BANG, my new partners made it clear on day one to keep my mouth shut and don't touch the radio. I was to listen for them to tell me what to do and not ask questions. I was their "mushroom." They kept me in the dark and fed me crap. Welcome to police work, Rookie.

Even though I was their mushroom, I knew the harder I worked the more respect and credibility I would gain.

Every day our mission was to arrest street-level drug dealers who sold on the street corners, in apartment complexes, party stores, and on vacant lots. We had to chase them down, find out where they got their dope, find out to whom they were selling it, and arrest as many people involved in the ring as possible. This ultimately led to drug raids. A lot of drug raids.

One of the corners in our district was Detroit Street/Coldwater. On the southwest side was the home of Sahiff's Party Store. Before we showed up, the dope thugs would fill the lot like ants. They were bold and fearless. They would approach cars whose occupants only came for a drink and chips and ask them if they wanted crack cocaine. It didn't matter if there were kids, elderly, or disabled people in the car; these maggots would try to sell dope to the pope.

On this particular day, we pulled quietly into the parking lot with our unmarked car. Donnie was driving, George next to him, and I was in the backseat. It wasn't long before my partners identified a group of guys dealing crack at the corner. Cars would stop at the light, and a hand-to-hand deal would go down. As we observed their activity, they finally saw us watching. We didn't care much because we wanted them to know they were being watched by "Johnny Law." They ended the operation and quickly got in their car parked behind the store. As they drove westbound on Coldwater, we tucked behind them. Speeds picked up, and, after a two-mile trek, they whipped southbound in a subdivision. Even I knew they were going to run. The car was barely in park when the doors flew open and all I saw were feet and elbows.

There were three of them and three of us. The front passenger and driver were held at gunpoint by Donnie and George. But the backseat passenger was the one who bolted toward the back of the house. He was my guy, and I was on his heels.

As we rounded the corner into the backyard, he reached his right hand into his waistband and pulled out a short-barreled pistol. Life went into slow motion. As he was turning the pistol towards me, I drew my.40 caliber Glock and aimed at his head. There was no way he was going to get the drop on Swanson. He saw that I had my gun aimed at him, and he must have realized that he had a greater chance of dying than killing me. He dropped his gun and kept running.

Remember this: In any high-crime urban environment, you don't want a loaded gun lying on the ground, so I slowed a step to pick it up and tried to secure it as I ran.

He moved from the backyard into the front yard, where he turned and charged me. With two guns in my hands, I'm not sure what he was thinking. But I couldn't shoot an unarmed man ... yet. I tried to holster my own gun, which is when my problem began. I had been wearing a piece-of-junk nylon holster that collapsed against my waist. With my hands full of guns, this dude jumped on me with "kill" in his eyes. I could now justify shooting an unarmed man. As we fought, I used my elbows, my knees, and my legs to fend him off. As I did, I glanced to my right to see Mt. Morris Township police officer, Denny Vanalstine. We called Denny "Wheels" because he was lightning fast. "Wheels" rounded the corner and body slammed my guy to the ground. That punk was now out of commission and in custody. Backup is awesome.

As soon as the suspect was secured in handcuffs, I dropped his gun, stepped on it, and finally secured my own gun in my piece-of-junk holster. A simple mistake— buying a junk holster that failed when I needed it—could have cost me my life. We cleared the scene, and all three bad guys were lodged in the Genesee County Jail. That was the last day I ever wore that holster. You may think the lesson here is about selling dope or foot chases. Not so.

_____

Impact Theme:

Always invest in the right gear, no matter if it's for sports, professional, or educational purposes.

Action Steps:

1. Plan ahead so that you know what you need in order to do the things you want to do properly.

2. Ask, read, and research experts in the areas you are interested in before you invest.

3. Invest in the best, whenever possible. Never skimp on quality when it comes to something that will get you ahead—or save your life.

3

The Day I Escaped Death

Countless homes and businesses are equipped with the most advanced burglar alarms on the planet. When a window or a door is disturbed, or if the house or business is actually broken into, those alarms are your best friend. However, more often than not, they are false alarms. Regardless of how often or why an alarm is triggered, when a call is dispatched to 911, an officer must respond.

It was a hot day in August when I was dispatched to an alarm at a farmhouse way outside the city limits. I didn't request backup because I thought I could handle it from the sound of the call; it didn't appear as though anyone was actually breaking into the house.

As I pulled in the driveway, I did a quick scan to see if I could find a vehicle that was out of place, a door cracked open, or a smashed window. I found nothing. I continued to scan the property as I got out of my patrol car and walked toward the home. I checked the home's windows as I moved tactically around the property. I was vigilant to make sure nobody had the chance to get the drop on me. Once the house perimeter was secure, I moved to the barns. There were two barns, one gigantic and the other a small feed barn. While searching the small barn, I heard sounds coming from the larger one.

My heart began to race. I started to move towards the main barn with my weapon drawn. As I got closer, I could hear shuffling inside.

I slowly turned a corner. My eyes were fixed on the inside, looking for the intruder. There he was. He looked at me, I looked at him, and I could see evil in his eyes. Under normal circumstances, I would have charged him, forced him to the ground, arrested him, and taken him to jail. But this suspect was much more dangerous than I had anticipated. As soon as our eyes met, he stepped toward me, and I had no choice but to run. I was taking no chances. I ran as fast as I could to my patrol car, knowing he was right on my tail. I could almost feel the evil in his heart as he ran, but he wasn't going to take ol' Swanson out. I grabbed the door handle of my car and pulled the door open, jumped inside, and slammed it shut. I was out of breath but thankful to be alive. He didn't give up. He started slamming into the driver-side door. I'm sure he wanted to kill me.

With backup a long way off, I decided to escape with my life and leave the scene. "Get back to your barn!" I screamed. It was like he could speak English. He turned and waddled away. The giant Tom turkey knew he ruled the roost!

It was the first and only time I'd ever retreated to my police car. However, I thought it was the best decision at the time; otherwise, shots would've been fired and there would have been bloodshed—and eventually meat and baked potatoes.

———————————————

Impact theme:

Be alert to your surroundings; you never know what kind of "intruder" will show up.

Action Steps:

1. Know who—and what—is around you at all times.

2. Stay alert.

3. Sometimes pulling back to regroup is the best option.

4

Merry Christmas, the Dog Just Ate Dad.

It was Christmas Eve, when silence was broken by the shooting at a home in the City of Grand Blanc. I arrived on scene, along with three other officers, just moments after the call was dispatched. I could hear screaming and the cries of children. We entered the front door and were stunned by what we saw. What was once peaceful and tranquil was now a war zone. The home had been decorated for Christmas. But now decorations were scattered and crushed throughout the living room. The Christmas tree was flipped over, and presents lay torn open on the floor. A trail of blood led us to the first bedroom, where three little kids huddled in terror. In the back bedroom was a dog, shot in the head. Off the bedroom was the back bathroom, where we found a wife standing next to her husband, screaming. He was lying in the tub with two broken arms. I could tell, without even touching him, he was going into shock and needed to get to the hospital five minutes ago.

Here's what happened moments before the 911 call was made.

The Christmas celebration was in full gear. Excitement hung in the air, and Santa would come soon. Dad began to roughhouse with the kids like every dad should. Mom came in from the kitchen, and Dad turned his attention toward her. He raised his hand, and his voice and moved toward her like a bear. It was all in fun ... or so everyone thought.

Everyone but the family dog, a full-grown bull mastiff. This kind of dog looks like a mini horse. Something snapped in this dog's head, and what was once a game turned violent. The dog must have thought Mom was under attack and he was going to protect her. It pounced out of the corner of the room and sank his teeth into the right arm of Dad. As his teeth buried into the deep tissue, with one shake of his massive head he broke the arm in half. Dad let out a bloody scream and everyone panicked, which made the dog even more insane. He went back at Dad's other arm and did the same thing, but this time didn't let go. The dog shook his head as though he wanted to rip off Dad's arm.

Dad screamed for his wife to grab the .22 caliber handgun in the dresser. She ran frantically to the bedroom and found the gun. It was unloaded. Screams continued to fill the air, which did not help the wife, who was still trying to load a small round into a revolver with trembling hands. Rounds fell to the floor. She persisted and was able to load one round and run toward the maniac dog, now dragging her husband to the back bedroom. She pointed the gun at the dog's head and fired. With that one shot, the giant beast fell and released its hold.

What happened, you ask? Well, the family pet acted on instinct, wanting to protect the woman, and did what it was born to do. Don't blame the dog.

Impact Theme:

Animals are always animals, and governed by instinct.

Respect them.

Action Steps:

1. You will never be able to take the instinct out of an animal. Never forget that.

2. Don't let fear paralyze you.

3. Sometimes doing the right thing can still have painful results.

A Pocket Full of Fish

I answered a 911 call in Flint Township about a suspicious man walking down the road. The caller described the male as having a disheveled look, long straggly blonde hair, and wearing a large camouflage jacket, dirty jeans, and army boots. The caller said the man had been going in and out of the businesses along the road asking questions that made no sense, freaking out both customers and staff.

Once I arrived at the area, it didn't take long before I found the man walking southbound on Elms Road. I thought he was possibly drunk, high, or mentally ill, all of which could be dangerous.

It was bitterly cold that morning, so I parked my cruiser behind him and approached, closely watching his hands and movements. When you are dealing with somebody like this, you have no idea what they are capable of or their intent. You have to learn how to talk their talk and know their language. I had to get into his world, and I did just that.

As I moved closer, I could tell this guy wasn't drunk or high. He was just emotionally disturbed. Someone who is mentally ill has a much different perception of reality. Remember, what is normal to me may be abnormal to him, and what's normal to him is abnormal to me. Not respecting his world could very easily lead to a physical confrontation.

I started talking to him, wanting to build some type of connection. I came up with whatever crazy thing I could think of to could create casual conversation. As I did, I moved in to check for weapons. I asked him to remove anything he had in his pockets, and he kept pulling out little pieces of paper: papers with people's names on them, phone numbers, and little written messages. What really stunned me was what he pulled out of his right front pocket: a pound of frozen tuna fish in a Ziploc bag.

When I first saw the tuna, I thought, *you've got to be kidding me.* But I knew it didn't matter whether it was a pound of tuna fish or a jar of mayonnaise. That tuna and those pieces of paper were the most important things this guy owned.

What he presented to me were really his life savings. Because I wanted to get into his head, what was important to him at that moment became important to me. I talked about how much I loved tuna fish. I told him I never thought about carrying a pound of it with me so perhaps when I get hungry, I could chunk off some tuna. It was a genius idea and he agreed. Now we were connecting.

As soon as I started recognizing and respecting his world, the stranger's hardness melted. I ended up giving him a ride to a friend's house. It might have been a lot different if I had confronted him, then criticized and demeaned his lifestyle. That doesn't do anything for anybody.

———————————

Impact Theme:

Treat people the way you would want to be treated, even if they have a pound of tuna in their pocket.

Action Steps:

1. Be kind to people even when they are different.

2. Learn to respect other people's values and seek to find common ground.

3. Always be aware of your surroundings, even when you feel comfortable. Normal situations can turn crazy, and crazy situations can turn normal. Be ready.

6

Dial 1-800 ...

I love doing traffic enforcement. It's not because I like to catch speeders; it's more that I like to catch people speeding who don't wear seat belts. That's my pet peeve.

I was driving southbound on Fenton Road when I saw a car approaching me in the opposite direction. I looked at my radar and I read 58 in a 45 mph zone. As the car passed me, I noticed that the driver was a single male driving a $50 car. I whipped my cruiser around, tucked in behind him, and prepared for the stop. He immediately slowed to the speed limit. I turned on my overhead lights and pulled him over on a side street. Most cops will tell you their decision to write a ticket is usually made even before they approach a vehicle. In this case, I was going to warn him because, as I approached, I could see he was wearing his seatbelt.

I walked to the driver's door and said my standard: "License, registration, and proof of insurance." He wasn't necessarily arrogant, but he certainly wasn't Mr. Friendly. I gathered his information and headed back to my car. I ran his info through my onboard computer to check for outstanding warrants. He had none.

I was about to head back to his car with a verbal warning when something caught my eye. *What is that? It can't be.* I noticed an interesting bumper sticker on the left side of his bumper. It read: if you don't like my driving, dial 1-800-EAT-****.

After writing a ticket for 10 over in a 45 mph zone, I went back to the driver. His arrogance was obvious, so I decided to have a little fun. "Excuse me, I tried to call the 1-800 number on the back of your bumper, but the line was busy. So you can take this ticket to your local magistrate to pay your fine. Oh, and slow down." As I turned away, I added, "And no, I don't like your driving."

Impact Theme:

Think through what you want to do. Ask yourself what message you want to send to those around you.

Action Steps:

1. Think of the long-term impact before you make big decisions.

2. Wait 24 hours before you commit.

3. Ask somebody close to you, and whom you respect, what they think of your decision ... and make sure you l-i-s-t-e-n.

7

Sometimes You Just Gotta Ask

Have you ever wondered if cops like traffic stops? Now before you answer, remember traffic stops and domestic disputes are the two most dangerous demands of a police officer.

We love traffic stops.

But we love them for different reasons.

Some cops pull cars over because they love giving tickets to soccer moms and old people. That's what gives cops a bad name. That's not me. Others love to pull cars over because it leads to outstanding warrants, guns, and dope. Now, that *is* me.

Not everybody deserves a ticket. Sometimes just the shock of being stopped can correct driver behavior. I know it does when *I* get pulled over.

When I make traffic stops, I confront many types of people. One afternoon I was working on Fenton Road, south of Hill in Grand Blanc, when I pulled over a vehicle doing 10 over. Whenever I pull over a vehicle, I have the same routine: I copy down the license plate on my clipboard, report it to the dispatcher, call in my location, and watch the movement inside the vehicle, before I even hit the lights. I study the vehicle to see how many occupants are inside. Strategizing my game plan, I decide if I should approach on the driver's side or the passenger side. *If it's nighttime, do I light up the car one way or another? How do I position my car?* These are questions every officer must answer before ever approaching a car.

After I pulled over the late model Buick with a single driver, I walked to the car with caution. I checked the trunk by shaking it to make sure it was closed and nobody was going to pop out.

I moved closer and looked in the backseat to see if someone was crouching down. I glanced in the passenger side and watched the hands of the driver. I know drivers are nervous and anxious for one reason or another. But so are the cops.

On that day, like many others, the first words out of my mouth were, "May I see your license, registration, and proof of insurance?" It's my own personal introduction. I don't say good morning. I don't say hello. I say nothing else.

On this stop, before I could get those words out, the driver turned to me with such innocent eyes, and said, "Please, please don't give me a ticket." Her voice told me she was desperate. To this day, I do not know what hit me other than she asked at the right time.

Without saying another word, I looked at the driver and said, "Okay." Then I turned and walked back to my cruiser.

I don't know if there was dope in the car or a dead body in the trunk. My gut told me no. Once I sat in my driver's seat, I could tell she was still stunned. After a few minutes, I drove away and lost her in my rear sights. I bet dollars to doughnuts (Yes, I used a doughnut reference) she's told that story 1,000 times.

In hindsight, I didn't go up there with the intent to give that person a break. It just hit me at the right time, just because she asked.

Impact Theme:
If you need something, anything, just ask.

Action Steps:
1. Be respectful even when you're caught.
2. Be courteous.
3. Live by the motto, "Pay it forward."

8

Where's Elmo?

I was taking a report on a DOA (dead on arrival) when dispatch redirected me to a medical call in Davison Township, almost 15 miles away. A 75-year-old man was having trouble breathing. While en route, I got held up by a train. As I waited, the call was upgraded to "the male now is not breathing," and CPR was in progress.

After the train cleared, it took me another 10 minutes to get to the scene. I found out later when the guy went down, his son—who had learned Cardio Pulmonary Resuscitation (CPR) 20 years prior as a lifeguard—had come from the basement, found his father unresponsive, and immediately started chest compressions.

As I pulled up on scene, the ambulance pulled in behind me.

In cardiac arrest, the key to resuscitation is to work the victim right where they are. It doesn't matter if it's in the middle of the street, a restaurant, or, in this case, the foyer of Elmo's house. As medics, we set up a mini emergency room (ER) right there.

Once the ambulance attendants took over the compressions from the victim's son, I did a quick look on the cardiac monitor. Bad news: there was no "shockable" rhythm. He was in asystole. I started an IV line to push fluids and cardiac medications. Then I focused on establishing an advanced airway. I took my intubation kit, placed the long metal blade in his mouth, lifted his tongue to the left, and inserted a plastic breathing tube in his trachea. This secures the airway and guarantees oxygen to the body and, most importantly, the brain. Breathing for the patient could now be handled externally.

Eighteen minutes after the patient went into cardiac arrest, we loaded him into the back of the ambulance.

He had yet to be shocked with the defibrillator. Once in the back of the rig, I looked at the monitor screen and could see there was a shockable rhythm. The cardiac meds I pushed earlier stimulated the heart muscle enough to generate some electrical impulses, which could hopefully be shocked into an organized, life-sustaining rhythm. I charged the defibrillator and delivered the first shock. It's like being smashed with a bat in the chest. But if it works, they get to live another day. I was in luck. Immediately his rhythm converted, and the man's eyes popped open.

I checked the pulse, both in the carotid artery and the radial artery, and he had both pulses. Just a few minutes after that, the endotracheal tube that I had placed, which triggers the gag reflex, caused him to gag. This told me he had brain activity—a great sign! Ten minutes later, I delivered him to the ER staff, then 45 minutes after I left the hospital.

Two years later, I was in my local Home Depot standing in line when a female in front of me turned around and asked if I was a deputy paramedic for the Sheriff's Office. Usually when that happens, it's because I wrote the person a ticket, or treated one of their loved ones. In this case, it was the latter.

She told me she was Elmo Campbell's daughter. I knew the name because when I resuscitated the guy in Davison Township, I remember filling out the name Elmo on my run sheet, which stood out to me. It was easy to remember since I have known only two Elmo's in my life, that man and the one from Sesame Street.

She told me after I resuscitated her dad that he was released from the hospital within the week, and had led a vibrant life for the past two years. Although he had just passed, I could see she was filled with joy by meeting me.

What I didn't know was that Elmo was not the man he should have been most of his life. It wasn't until he was given a second chance that day he made peace with people he offended, and he forgave people who needed to be forgiven. He became more tolerant. He loved more and lived more. In those two years, she told me, they did more together as a family than ever before.

How awesome is that?

I humbly reminded her that what I did was "cookbook medicine." Any medic with half a brain would have done the same thing, but I was glad it had been me. What really made the difference, however, was her brother's CPR. He kept the window of opportunity open for me to do what I was trained to do. Without him, Elmo would have been taken to the funeral home that day. I gave her a big ole' hug and walked away thinking I would never see her again.

Soon after, I was promoted to detective/sergeant and was sitting in my detective bureau cubicle. A call came over the radio: A car had just hit a tree. A man driving to work had slid on ice, throwing his car into a spin and slamming into the tree. He died on impact.

It was Elmo's son.

The one who gave his dad CPR.

I felt so bad for the family that I broke protocol of not going to visitations or funerals for people I know from my job. But this time, I felt compelled to give my condolences to the family.

As I walked into the Hanson Funeral Home in downtown Davison, Elmo's wife, and the daughter whom I had met at Home Depot, ran up to me and gave me a heartfelt hug. I told them I wanted to show my support because of the impact their family had on me. In mid-sentence she hurried me back to a little room off the main chapel. There I saw an 8x10 framed picture on a small coffee table. It was the portrait of Elmo, his wife, and their 10 grown children.

Elmo's wife told me that once he was released from the hospital, they made it a point to have this one and only family photo of their adult family. Now that Elmo and his son were both gone, they would never have that opportunity again. What they would have, however, is the memory of a restored family and a picture to memorialize it. I was honored. We ended our short visit, and I quietly slipped out the rear exit.

I love being a medic. When I arrive on a call, I want them to know without question they having nothing to worry about, even if they do. I may not be the best medic, but I am *their* medic.

———————————————

Impact Theme:
Do what you love and do it well; you never know the impact you will have on others.

Action Steps:
1. Serve others. Things you do today might restore their tomorrow.
2. Your best effort is *not* an option; always give it.
3. Keep a servant attitude; you never know when you'll be needed.

9

This I've Never Seen!

I was dispatched to a shooting in the north end of Genesee County. As the scene details unfolded, I realized it was probably a self-inflicted gunshot wound to the head.

I parked my cruiser with caution in front of an old two-story, rundown apartment complex. My cop instincts engaged. Whenever there's a shooting, you want to make sure the scene is secured before anybody is treated. Scene safety, police safety, and bystander safety is key when it comes to any violent encounter. The other officers and I carefully entered the apartment building to lock down the scene and make sure there were no other victims—or shooters.

As I walked into the front apartment, I noticed a side stairway that led to the upstairs room where we were told the shooting occurred. I was met halfway by a giant of a man coming down the stairs toward us. He was the gnarly, long-haired, bearded, sleeve-tattooed son of the victim. As he passed, we did a quick pat down for weapons since he was the kind of guy that if someone were to be shot, he could do it. (Yes, I'm judging. I was there, so relax.) We ordered his hands high. I could tell he wasn't aggressive but rather distraught. We quickly secured him and made sure he was out of the apartment before going any further.

We continued upstairs, then I went to the left and slowly opened the door that led to the living room. Using my left hand, with my gun in the right, I pushed the old wooden door ajar. As it slowly creaked open, I could see a man sitting in a chair with his back to me. "Let me see your hands!" I yelled. No movement. I repeated my command. Still nothing. As I got closer, I could see he was a grey-haired gentleman wearing a red flannel shirt and blue jeans, and gripping a small caliber pistol in his right hand. He never moved or responded. I made my way to the front of his chair, then realized why.

He was dead.

The scene was secure. We had time on our side, so I turned to examine the body more closely. Black powder burns from the shot were embedded in the middle of his forehead. This "tattooing" denotes that the barrel of the weapon was close to the skin, if not directly pushed into the surface of the skin when the gun was fired. This happens when the gunpowder inside the bullet carriage is ignited by the spark of the hammer pin. The explosion propels the bullet itself down the barrel, along with flaming hot gunpowder causing the burns.

On the surface, it appeared to be a suicide. The son acted appropriately, and the quick scene investigation confirmed the "obvious." But obvious can be wrong. A witness below the apartment told us she heard two shots, then the screams of the son. Two shots.

I decided to look at the corpse even closer. Upon further examination, I noticed why she heard two shots. Not only was there a hole in his forehead, but there was another shot to his chest directly into his heart. Two fatal shots!

I yelled to my partners, "Hey, keep that son in custody. This isn't right." Still, the son was acting appropriately. His responses and his psychological demeanor indicated this was just a suicide. But how?

The detectives arrived and came to the same conclusion as I did: Something was wrong. We now had to rely on the forensic pathologist to determine what had happened. The body was transported to the morgue and scheduled for an autopsy the next day.

I made certain I was there for the autopsy in an effort to settle my curiosity. The next day I arrived at Hurley Medical Center Morgue. It's a cold, dark room filled with the constant stench of decomposition and cold coffee. Off to the left is an oversized walk-in cooler where the dead are secured in white body bags awaiting their own examination.

An autopsy starts with an external exam, photos, and measurements. Front side and then the rear. Any clothing or other hints of evidence are secured in evidence bags and labeled. Sitting next to the body is a hanging scale with a large stainless steel basin and a thick plastic bag formed inside.

The cutting begins at the chest, where the pathologist makes a large incision over both sides of the ribcage. Transitioning to the bone saw, they cut through the ribs and remove the front ribcage. The layers of the tissue covering the heart and lungs are also removed. Each organ is spread over a cutting board, where it is physically examined. A small cross section is taken via scalpel, and the rest was placed into the stainless steel basin already set up. As the organs are placed, they are weighed in grams and recorded. One by one, all the organs are treated the same way and placed in the scale. The weight is recorded each time a new organ is added to the basin by simply noting the weight before and subtracting the weight after the organ is placed. From the chest to the stomach, they are all removed and end up in the bag. As the internal cavity is emptied, blood and urine samples are taken, then placed into vials and labeled for toxicological testing.

Now to the head.

A long cut is made from ear to ear in the back of the scalp against the skull bone. The skin is then pulled back and tucked underneath the front of the chin. Yes, you heard me correctly, the skin is pulled all the way from the back of the head to the front. Here comes the bone saw again. A circular saw cut is made, and two stainless steel wedges are pressed in on each side. With a quick twist of the hand, "pop" the skull cap comes off. The brain is cut free and removed, examined and weighed, then, yep—in the bag. All this takes about 45 minutes depending on the presumed cause of death. Once this stage is complete, there is only a shell of a body lying next to a steel basin. The skull cap is placed on the top of the skull, the skin is pulled back, and then stapled in place. The pathologist then places the entire plastic bag and all contents inside the chest cavity, where the rib cage protects the bag. Finally, the skin is pulled tight across the chest and stapled securely. The body is rinsed once again, then released to the funeral home for final preparations. It's a bit much to take in until you get used to it. But each piece of the puzzle helps indicate what happened to the body.

 Here's what happened.

This poor dude found a.32 caliber handgun and shot himself in the forehead. The problem was he used a low velocity.32-caliber junk round, or what is known as a full metal jacket. As the bullet left the barrel, it travelled between both hemispheres of his brain and lodged in the back of the skull, never touching an ounce of brain tissue. It caused no trauma, other than an incredible headache and a hole in the front of his skull.

After the first shot didn't work, he shot himself in the chest, which lodged in his heart.

Manner of death: suicide. Cause of death: gunshot wound to the chest.

———————————————

Impact Theme:

Be careful; not everything is what it appears.

Action Steps:

1. Dig deeper to find the truth.

2. Go with your gut. Always look below the surface to find the truth.

3. Bring in more experts to find the truth.

-10-

The Most Expensive Lunch Ever

In 1978, the Genesee County Sheriff's Office in Flint, Michigan, started a program through a federal grant that deployed deputies who were certified police officers and cross-trained them as licensed paramedics. The grant called for them to drive police cruisers and carry emergency medical gear such as IV Fluids, narcotics, cardiac drugs, advanced airway equipment, and surgical utensils. We called ourselves "Echo Units."

Echo Units are virtually emergency room physicians with a gun. They are dispatched to 911 calls that require a police officer and also demand the service of a licensed advanced life support paramedic.

I became a licensed paramedic in 1993 after nearly two years of paramedic school at our local trauma center. Once I finished medic school, I was sent to the Delta

Police Academy in Saginaw, Michigan. After graduating from the police academy, I officially became an Echo Unit with the Office of Genesee County Sheriff.

I was working second shift, 3:00 p.m. to 11:00 p.m., when dispatch sent me to a personal injury accident in Vienna Township.

A grandpa made a left-hand turn out of a McDonald's, and his car was hit on the passenger side by an oncoming car. The 14-year-old grandson took the full impact.

When I arrived on scene, I could see the right side of the vehicle was crushed and the boy had smashed his head on the A post, which is the piece of structural metal that goes between the front passenger window and the windshield. Firefighters were actively using the Jaws of Life to extricate the boy from the twisted metal. The boy was struggling to breathe as we pulled him out and placed him on the hard plastic backboard. My partner, Doug, and I lifted the backboard and secured the young victim on the stretcher just outside the crowd of responders. Upon closer inspection, I could see the right side of this kid's head was caved in. His pulse weakened by the minute, his breathing labored and irregular. When this happens in trauma situations, people quickly die.

We loaded the grandson into the ambulance and headed towards one of the best trauma hospitals in the nation, Hurley Medical Center. On the way, the boy's heart failed. Then he stopped breathing. He was in complete cardiac arrest.

Doug and I alternated doing chest compressions as the ambulance swayed back and forth from the high speeds. I put an intubation tube into the boy's trachea that allowed us to breathe for him. IV lines were hooked up to help replace the fluids lost from the internal injuries. We were trying everything to bring this kid back. Then came a clear sign of impending death: brain matter coming from his left nostril. It's what we call a significant mechanism of injury. But our valiant effort to stabilize his precious body never wavered. Fifteen minutes later, we pulled into the ER. They saw what we saw, and it wasn't very long before all of us knew his little body wouldn't revive. That's it; his life was over in an instant, and all he wanted just minutes before was a McDonald's lunch with Grandpa. I finished my run report, restocked my jump kit with the fluids and needles I used on my young patient, and checked back into service ready for another tragedy. I know it sounds callous, but in this business tragedy never stops.

Impact Theme:

Appreciate life NOW!

Action Steps:

1. Live like there's no tomorrow by doing what's important today.

2. Live like this is your best day. Wake up appreciating what you have, not dwelling on what you don't.

3. Decide every day to DO. Don't sit around!

11

Running From Jesus

I was working midnights and stopped home at 2:00 a.m. to check on my wife, who was pregnant with our first child. While there, I heard a call go out for a "breaking and entering" five miles west of my location. As the officers responded, one of them saw the suspect pull out of the victim's driveway and flee at a high speed northbound. This was now a legit police chase, "As Seen on TV."

Let me be honest: Cops love chasing bad people. If you could watch from above, you would see police cars from across the county do everything in their power to put themselves in a position to get involved. This is not always the best idea, but it is reality nonetheless.

Police chases are also dangerous and controversial, but in some circumstances, they are necessary.

After the suspect car went northbound for two miles, it turned east towards my direction. I quickly kissed my wife goodbye and jumped in my patrol car. Now only three miles away, I began paralleling the vehicle on another road, guessing the route the guy might go. It's purely a game of luck, and it could be a game of bad luck.

The traffic was light, the roads were clear, and I wanted to get this guy. As I turned west, I knew that if he made another turn south, he'd come right to me.

And that's exactly what he did.

Now we were head-on. I was northbound and he was now southbound. As he was coming at me, I crossed over to head into his lane, wanting him to swerve and crash into the ditch. It didn't work. At the last second, I went to the right and he went left, just like the old-fashioned chicken game. I made a quick 180 degree turn, which allowed me to become the primary car in the chase, and I got right on his tail.

Less than a quarter mile later, he turned into the Good Shepherd Lutheran Church, whose parking lot was secured with gates. That didn't stop him. He drove around the gates, through the drainage ditch, toward the back parking lot and into a grassy field. Spinning out behind the houses, the man jumped out of his car and ran. I was on him like peanut butter on jelly. All this happened within seconds.

It was just me and him. I tackled him in the field, and we began to fight. With fists flying, it wasn't long before I shoved his hands behind his back and cuffed him.

Once he was secured, I quickly realized I wasn't alone. Nope. There was a spectator. The chase and the fight all took place just 15 feet away from the home of Pastor Ewald, the pastor of the Good Shepherd Lutheran Church. He told me later that he had been jolted awake and jumped out of bed to see what was happening. He watched the entire incident unfold: the cars, the dirt, the fists, and the fight.

It just so happened that I knew the pastor personally. He had presided over the wedding of my sister and her husband just a few years prior. Standing before me with a shocked look plastered on his face, I said the only thing I thought appropriate at the time: "Pastor, this guy ran from Jesus, and now he's going to jail."

_____

Impact Theme:
No matter where you are or what you are doing, somebody is watching.

Action Steps:
1. Be aware of your surroundings.
2. Don't quit fighting. You can win.
3. Live by the motto: "Nothing to hide, nothing to fear."

12

I'm *Not* That Person

My wife, Jamie, and I were celebrating our anniversary in the town of Frankenmuth, just 30 miles north of where we live. As we drove through the town, I caught the eye of a Frankenmuth police officer, and he started following me. He was about to disrupt my evening. I watched through the rearview mirror and noticed he was running my plate. I wasn't speeding, and I wondered why he was following me. We drove another mile until I pulled into the bakery of a well-known resort. When he pulled behind us, I told Jamie, "We are going to get stopped."

As I parked and started to get out of the car, he moved his car at an angle and hit his lights. I was already half way out of my truck, so I made sure I told him, "I am Chris Swanson, a police officer, and I have a weapon." No response. Not even a look.

Tactical mistake #1: The officer was told I had a gun, but he didn't even acknowledge what I said.

Jamie also got out of the car. It was almost as if I didn't exist. The officer ignored me and completely locked eyes with Jamie. "Are you Jamie Swanson?" he asked.

"Y ... yes ... I am."

"Will you come here, please?" He still had not acknowledged me or the fact that I just told him I had a gun. She walked to his car and, as she did, I reached into my left pocket to pull out my wallet to get my police identification.

Tactical mistake #2:The officer should have never let me reach into my pocket after I told him I had a gun.

As I fumbled for my ID in my wallet, it fell to the ground, scattering the contents everywhere. I bent down to pick them up; as I did, I could hear the officer and my wife talking but couldn't make out the conversation. I stood up to put my cards back when I saw a look on my wife's face that I had never seen before. She said, "Chris, he wants me to get in the back of his police car."

"What?" I yelled.

As I approached this officer, I became more stern and deliberate in my tone. "Wait a second. She is not getting in the back of your car."

Tactical Mistake #3: The officer should never let me approach, knowing I had a gun.

"Listen," he said, "she's got a warrant for her arrest, and she's getting in my car."

"For what?" I asked with disgust.

"She is wanted out of Grand Traverse County for writing a bad check," he replied.

How could this be true? Maybe she mistakenly wrote a check on a vacation and made an accounting error. No way! You need to know that Jamie is a social worker and a tenderhearted, Proverbs 31 woman. She is also the most organized numbers chic I've ever met. Ain't no way she wrote a bad check.

Again, she refused to get in the car, and the verbal confrontation escalated. I told the officer I was a sergeant at the sheriff's office, this was my wife, and I needed to know what he was talking about before she was going to do anything.

He explained that while he was following me, he ran the license plate of my SUV, and it came back to Jamie Lynne Swanson with a misdemeanor warrant for her arrest. I asked him the date of birth, the month, and the day. He gave me her proper birthday, but obviously something was still wrong. Something triggered me to ask to see the in-car computer, which he surprisingly allowed. He had still not checked my identification, nor searched me.

Tactical Mistake #4: The officer should have made sure he knew what he was talking about before telling someone he had a warrant for their arrest.

His search came back as a Jamie Lynn Swanson, but with no "E" on the Lynn, and the same birthday. It was starting to make sense. My Jamie has an "E" at the end of her middle name.

I let out a deep breath and told him, "Let me see the address associated with this person." Again, he let me look into his cruiser and read the address on his computer. It was not our address.

Jamie was still standing outside the police car, exasperated and scared.

I called the sheriff's office that entered the warrant in Grand Traverse County to confirm the warrant was not for *my* Jamie. After 20 minutes of sorting out the confusion, my wife was dismissed from her "arrest." I can't say my law enforcement colleague and I left on the best of terms. He had a job to do, like me, but he was terrible at it.

But there's more ...

Later that night, when emotions were calm, Jamie whispered she wanted to confess something to me. She told me she wasn't as nervous about getting stopped and having an alleged warrant. She was more nervous about getting in the back of the police car. She had seen that very scene in a movie, and thought that perhaps there was some type of conspiracy going on. Worse yet, she thought that maybe this officer was trying to save her because her husband (me) was living the secret life of a serial killer.

Can you believe that?

I convinced my wife that I was not a serial killer, but after her comments, I thought about starting now.

Impact Theme:

Be persistent.

Action Steps:

1. Keep good records.

2. Stand for what's right.

3. Dig into the details.

13

The Craigslist Criminals

I had just returned to work from a four-day Memorial Day weekend. While reviewing the weekend activity reports, I saw the Auto Theft Unit had reported multiple carjacking's in the city of Flint. But these were unique. These particular crimes involved victims who had contacted individuals selling iPhones on Craigslist. Here's how they got jacked.

A willing buyer looking to buy an iPhone would find an ad on Craigslist—advertising iPhones being sold cheap, way cheap—not knowing it was fake. They would call and get the details. Unbeknownst to them, their call was to street thugs. The thugs would tell them, "Yup, we've got iPhones for sale. $150 each or two for $200 and bring cash."

Greed overshadowed common sense, and the soon-to-be victims would agree to the deal and meet the thugs at

Longfellow School parking lot in the city. Blinded by their excitement to get a great deal, they would bring the $200 cash and drive to the school, where the criminals waited to pounce.

Three suspects would approach the car, one in the front, one at the passenger side, and one at the driver's door. They would all have backpacks. The one at the driver side would either open the door, or the person inside would roll down the window. The thugs would ask, "Can I help you?"

The victim inside would innocently respond, "I'm supposed to meet someone here to buy an iPhone."

As soon as they heard that, the thugs pulled their pistols and held the person at gunpoint. They would take their money and their car, leaving the victim stranded and paralyzed with fear. This happened four times over the weekend.

I knew this would be a great undercover sting operation, if we could set it up and use the thug's bait against them.

Lt. Kevin Shanlian of the GAIN Unit of auto theft came up with the plan. We called the suspects ourselves and ordered our two iPhones. We had one goal in mind: draw these thugs out and give them a taste of their own medicine.

We chose a female officer to make the order in an attempt to keep the thugs' guard down, as most of the weekend's victims had been females. Within a few hours, the thugs had called the undercover officer back and set up the exchange using the same parking lot as per the other victims. Once the call was made, we sat and waited. The other undercover officers and I were parked in abandoned houses, driveways, or were hidden behind overgrown bushes.

More than an hour passed before we spotted three male suspects approaching from the south side of the field toward our officer's vehicle. If the deal was made, our undercover officer was to simply speed away once she knew these were the correct suspects. This was a dangerous operation. The only way for our undercover to know the real suspects was to wait until a gun was stuck in her face.

As the thugs moved closer, everyone held their positions. The suspects approached the car just like the previous victims described, one to the front, one to the side, and one at the driver window. From my vantage point, I could see they pulled out a pistol and leveled it at her head. As planned, our undercover officer sped away. The deal was done. "Go, go, go!" the radio traffic screamed.

Our team swarmed the suspects from all directions, with engines racing and tires screeching. I drove my four-wheel-drive Chevy Tahoe through the field chasing after one of the suspects, who dropped his bag and fled. As I was chasing him, another marked cruiser, a canine unit driven by Sergeant Jeff Antcliff, flew from the opposite side of the field, and we pinned the suspect between his cruiser and a tree. I jumped out of my Tahoe, grabbed hold of him, flipped him over the hood to the ground, then handcuffed him. The other two suspects were also arrested.

All three thugs were charged with armed robbery, carjacking, and felony firearm. It was great police work from start to finish. Not often do plans such as these work out so smoothly. The cops were safe and the bad guys went to jail.

Impact Theme:
Don't get blinded by greed.

Action Steps:
1. Don't respond on emotion; keep your selfishness in check.
2. Investigate all opportunities carefully.
3. Don't be naïve to the real-world dangers.

14

Peach Pie and Gunfire

It was two days before Thanksgiving when they returned to his house from a day of shopping and a romantic dinner out. She was quickly becoming his new love interest. Life couldn't get any better—or so they thought. The new couple sat quietly at the kitchen table, sharing a freshly warmed piece of peach pie, illuminated by the dim light over the kitchen table. I'm sure they recounted the day and their future together.

If you watched the scene from the outside, amidst the darkness of the night, you could see love and would know they had a bright future ahead. In fact that is exactly what the woman's ex-husband was doing. He was outside watching them through the big picture window, armed with two handguns and extra magazines of ammunition. His marriage to the woman had ended five years prior, but his rage and jealousy never did. He had stalked the loving couple all day. Earlier in the evening, the ex-husband parked his car a mile down the road and walked to the house. As he stood and stared, his rage consumed him. The happy couple's world was about to be shattered.

At the point when he couldn't stand it anymore, he pulled his first handgun from the holster, stood six feet from the window in the dark of night, and fired his weapon. The shots stunned the two inside as they dove to the floor. Shots continued to ring out as glass and drywall littered the room around them. The two managed to run to the stairway, then to an upstairs bedroom, slammed the door, and called 911. Outside, the shooter continued to fire. He emptied one magazine and reloaded. Then he entered the home through the picture window.

Shouts and threats of death from the ex-husband filled the air. As the 911 dispatcher gathered more information from the new boyfriend, she simultaneously dispatched the police and did all she could to calm the situation. What the dispatcher didn't know was that the new boyfriend was a big game hunter and had loaded a Remington .270 caliber rifle. He was able to kill anyone who came through his bedroom door.

"If this guy opens the door, I'm going to kill him," he told the dispatcher. Sure enough, dispatch recorded the manic shouts of the gunman screaming as he climbed the stairs. Step-by-step he moved toward the bedroom door. He grabbed the handle and opened the door. He then met a greater force than he had anticipated—the calm and collected hunter and his rifle.

One Shot. One Kill. Crisis over.

The couple calmly stepped over the warm corpse and headed down the stairs to await the police.

After some time, I arrived on scene to investigate. The medics had already taken the ex-husband to the hospital, even though he was expected to remain dead, given half his chest was in the bedroom. I did a quick field interview of the two victims on the first floor and could tell they had nothing to hide. I walked through the scene, still filled with the smell of stale gunpowder. Broken glass covered the floor like a new snowfall. On the table was a perfectly positioned, half-eaten, warm piece of peach pie, the remnants of a once-quiet evening.

As the investigation continued, it was confirmed the ex-husband had been violent for the last five years. He had been causing unbelievable havoc in his former wife's life. But after being interviewed at our office telling the same story I've just relayed to you, they were returned to the house to begin picking up the pieces of their lives— literally.

The prosecutor later ruled the shooting was self-defense and cleared the Big Game Hunter.

Case Closed.

_____

Impact theme:
Be aware of the chaos that might be lurking around you.

Action Steps:

1. Always have an exit plan if danger strikes.

2. Be ready, be prepared.

3. Stay calm and protect yourself.

-15-

"Jack!"

In the spring of 2001, there was an elderly lady killed in Lapeer, Michigan, a county just to the east of mine.

It was a brutal killing. They dragged her out of the house, tortured her, and left her to die in a ditch. The suspects were beyond armed and dangerous. They were evil. One of the suspects was a Latino who lived on the east side of Flint. We were asked by the Lapeer County Sheriff Office to assist in finding the suspect. Using anonymous tips, confidential informants, and surveillance, we had a possible suspect and location. His name was Francisco and he was a stone-cold killer.

Francisco grew up on the east side under horrific conditions. His family were members of the organized gang called the Spanish Cobras. His brothers and sisters were either in the dope business or prostitution. He had very little chance of succeeding in life. Trying to get him and make the charges stick took time.

Using an informant, the day came to raid what we thought was the target house. The information from the informant made the search warrant valid. However, when receiving such information, there are two things to remember. First, informants are still criminals. Second, their information is not always correct. Verify!

We were given a description of the home we were going to raid. We drove the informant past the home to confirm the address one more time, and the description of the house was added to the search warrant. The rest of the team headed back to the Sheriff's Office to develop a detailed raid plan.

Once the plan had been finalized, all undercover officers reported to their cars and made their way to the target house. There were three teams: one for the main floor, one for the basement, and one for the upstairs.

I led the team to the upstairs. We smashed down the front door at approximately 1:30 a.m. and announced: "Police! Search warrant!" We heard nothing. My team ran up the stairs to secure the top floor.

I could hear the other officers clearing the bottom floors and the basement. Once upstairs, we were confronted with three doors that were shut.

The first choice was the door to the right. I held my Remington Model 870 12 gauge shotgun aimed at the door as I advanced. I booted the door open, and there in the bed resting comfortably was who I thought was the suspect. I leveled my shotgun, ordered him to get up, and announced that we were the police. As the startled suspect rose, I could quickly tell this older white dude was *not* Francisco. Our eyes met and my mind said, *I know this guy!*

With hands up and eyes wide, the man spoke words that I will never forget: "Chris, is that you?"

Uh-oh!

My eyes fixated on him as I tried to process how the heck he knew my name. Then it hit me. It's Jack! A deacon from my church! We hit the wrong house.

I wanted to crawl out of that room faster than humanly possible. Thank the Lord that Jack was gracious. We explained what we had done, fixed his door, and to this day, whenever I see Jack, I always tell him he has the key to the city. In any other circumstances the city would still be paying. God bless Jack!

The address we were supposed to hit was next to Jack's. The building was a split unit, and we were supposed to hit the left unit.

Eventually, Francisco was arrested and is now resting comfortably in prison.

_____

Impact Theme:
Small details matter.

Action Steps:

1. Check, double check, triple check.

2. Don't ever assume.

3. Be thankful for the grace shown by others when you make a mistake, and do the same.

I love you, Jack!

16

Your Daddy Was the BEST Ever

It was a beautiful September evening when I got a phone call around 11:30 p.m. One of my sergeants, a friend of mine, got arrested by another police agency. He was drinking when he got into a fight with his wife, so they tossed him in jail.

My sergeant friend was assigned to the patrol division with our office. However, I had no empathy. I figured whatever he does, or whatever he did, it was on him. He'll have to figure it out himself.

Just a few hours later, around 3:00 a.m., he called my house after he was released from jail. He said, "Sir, I apologize. I made some bad decisions, and I am going to own it."

"You know what, you better figure out why you were so stupid," I fired back. "This isn't you, man. You're better than that. You have more self-control than to put yourself in such a bad position, and it's going to be you that has to get you out of it."

He agreed.

I told him that if he were serious about getting help, he should meet me the next day at the office, and we would get a game plan for restoration. Sure enough, he did. We talked about his demon of drinking. We talked about things that were going on, and I invited him to church that Sunday. He enjoyed the service, asked questions, and began to attend regularly. He also started to build a relationship with our pastor. It wasn't long before he made a decision to accept Jesus in his life. I was there. I saw it live.

He was now on a great path—or so I thought. Yet something strange continued to occur. Throughout the following months, more and more unusual activity happened to his now ex-wife: suspicious destruction of her cars and her property, nasty phone calls, and more.

As time passed, my sergeant continued to perform his normal day-to-day duties without missing a beat, and nothing seemed out of the ordinary.

Almost a year to the day, I received another late-night phone call, but this one was in a panic. It was 11:00 p.m. and my lieutenant, who was the on-duty administrator, called to inform me that my sergeant had gotten drunk and thought it would be a great idea to drive to his ex-wife's apartment and smash her car with a bat. A couple of minutes into his outrage, the local police responded and confronted him. He had a decision to make: cooperate or not.

Sadly, he chose option #2.

He jumped into his truck and made a bad situation much worse. Speeds reached 100 mph before my sergeant pulled into a driveway to back up and head the other way, with a police car right behind him. He smash into the front of the car, then drove forward through the yard.

My heart sank. I jumped out of bed, got dressed, hopped into my unmarked police car parked in my garage, and listened to the radio. I tried to call my sergeant on his phone multiple times, but it went to voicemail.

I could hear the chase being called minute-by-minute, with speeds faster and faster. My sergeant was on a rampage. He didn't stop at a single light or sign. What was crazy was just seven hours before, he had been on-duty in uniform at our office.

Listening to the blow-by-blow of the chase over the radio, I heard he drove on the expressway southbound at US 23 at Grand Blanc Rd. I felt helpless. As he got off the expressway to turn around to evade the officers, he took the next exit, which was too sharp. His truck rolled and he was ejected. When the truck came to a stop, it was right on top of his sprawled-out body, crushing his chest. I then headed to the scene.

Over the radio, I heard that the first officer at the crash site location was a Michigan State trooper. He notified dispatch that he watched the ejection and it looked like the driver was dead. Our paramedics soon arrived and started CPR and Advanced Life Support. Then they loaded him in the ambulance and raced to the trauma center.

I diverted and headed to the hospital. When I arrived, I alerted the staff that one of our own was coming. At first, the trauma staff didn't realize I meant a police officer. I repeated myself, then they got it. I watched the ambulance speeding down the driveway, lights on, and police cars following. When the ambulance came to a stop, I opened the back door and saw the shell of my friend. He had very few external injuries, but I knew, because of the speed and how he was ejected, his insides were destroyed.

The crew moved quickly to trauma bay #1, and I watched the hospital staff work tirelessly trying to resuscitate him. Fifteen minutes later, we all knew there was no hope. At 12:01 a.m. on October 1, 2008, my sergeant, my friend, was pronounced dead.

It gets so quiet in the emergency room when someone is pronounced dead. Nobody talks. No more ventilator. No oxygen flowing. No suction, no rhythmic cardiac monitor sounds. Just quiet.

The silence is deafening.

Even though I knew it was him, I had to make sure, so I looked at the tattoos on the backs of his arms. He had his boys' names on them. I know his boys. It was truly him … I just didn't want to believe it.

As if this couldn't get any worse, his mother was on the way. I knew it was going to be hard for her because years ago the sergeant's dad, her husband, died the exact same way: a car accident. Now this poor woman had lost her son.

When she walked into the grieving room, I was waiting for her. The weeping came from her gut. Her tears fell like rain. She buried her head in my chest.

As the days progressed, I offered to be a liaison between his ex-wife and the family. Due to the dynamics, they took me up on the offer. I kept in contact with the mother, and I was there to assist in the funeral arrangements. I wanted to make sure everyone was cordial and civil. They picked out the casket, the grave site, and the service details. Despite his bad acts he was my friend, and I wanted to make sure he got the personal touch.

As a police officer, I felt he still deserved basic police honors. I am not proud of how he died, just how he lived for the people he protected. At the sheriff's office, I command the honor guard. My sergeant was one of our members and would be buried in his honor guard uniform. Every day before visitation, I would go to the funeral home and inspect him in his casket. I wanted to make sure his brass was shined, his buttons straight, and nothing out of order. Alive, he looked like he was chiseled out of marble. He just looked the part: not a wrinkle in his uniform, big, strong, and tall. He deserved the same honor in death.

The funeral was on a Monday. I went to the funeral home before anybody arrived to inspect him one last time. I noticed a trickle of fluid from his autopsy incision. When I asked the funeral director to clean it up, he didn't hesitate. I also removed the backings of his collar brass and unclipped his badge. I removed his nameplate and laid it on his chest. I would give these to his family at the conclusion of the service. Our pastor who led him to the Lord one year prior conducted the funeral service and delivered a great gospel message, impacting the crowd of cops, family, and friends. Then it was time for the honor guard.

My sergeant was my number six in the firing line of our seven-man rifle detail. Now he was gone. As the remaining honor guard marched to the casket, the number six spot was occupied by a four foot pedestal on which rested his boots, his hat, and his gloves. Anytime we do a rifle detail, I walk the line to inspect and make sure that everything's in order. In this case, I stopped at number six. I turned, rendered honors with a hand salute, and continued on to number seven.

After inspecting the last honor guard, I backed up to the casket, removed the brass, the badge, and the nameplate, which I had loosened earlier in the day. I turned to his ex-wife seated next to their beautiful boys. I took my hat off and opened up her hand to give her his badge and brass. With a softball-size lump in my throat, I knelt down in front of the boys and said, "Your daddy was the best police officer that ever lived. Don't ever forget that."

I wanted to say more but couldn't. I wanted to cry my pain and anger away, but crying is not an option when you serve in the honor guard.

I stood to my feet, put my hat back on, glanced at the boys, and thought, *What's that brass and badge going to do when those boys walk down the aisle of their high school commencement, and they are looking for their dad? What's that badge going to do when their first love breaks up with them, and they need comfort from their dad? What's that badge going to do when they get married, and they want to see their dad?*

Nothing!

I got mad.

Even though I loved him as a brother, his bad decisions cost deeply. His decision to accept Christ in his life could have been a true turning point. But, like all of us, turning points only become positive when we choose to walk down the right road.

His decisions will impact people for generations. My sergeant is buried in a grave and every May 15, National Police Officer Day, I visit him and we talk.

_____

Impact Theme:

The decisions we make can have serious repercussions with real consequences. Never forget that and make wise ones!

Action Steps:

1. Be aware of what you're doing, and how your actions impact others.
2. Don't choose to do something that you know will hurt others.
3. If you screw up, fix it, forgive, and move on.

17

Finding Ernie

"Brother, if there were anyone who could help me, I was told you could."

"Who is this?" I asked.

The broken voice replied, "My name is Ernesto."

Ernesto was a local pastor whose friend convinced him to try one more time to connect the dots that could restore the family.

"Alright, Ernesto, how can I help?"

He told me that he and his brother Antonio grew up on the east side of Flint after they left Texas as young kids. For years he had desired to find his father, who walked out over 25 years ago. I could tell by his voice this was a long and brokenhearted battle.

 "What's the last memory you have of your father?" I asked.

"Only a silhouette when I was five years old as he kissed me goodnight and quietly walked out of my bedroom, never to be seen again," he whispered softly.

My heart filled with pain for him.

At the time, I was the captain of the law enforcement agency with years of investigative experience under my belt. I figured Ernesto's phone call had probably been preplanned for many weeks and maybe even months, in order for him to get the courage to call me. Ernesto told me he had wanted to find his father for years and made many attempts over the years. But now he needed more help. He was desperate and wounded. I wanted to help but wasn't sure I could.

As the conversation continued, Ernesto unburdened more than 30 years of pain. But I needed more information. I asked for his father's full name, last known city and state, and any anything else I could cross-reference. All he had was a name, Ernesto Alaniz, Sr., a 58-year-old Mexican from Corpus Christi, Texas. That's it. I promised Ernesto I would do what I could to help. After concluding our emotional exchange, I went to work.

Detectives are in the business of finding people. Using the knowledge, tools, and experience from years of service, we can find you. In a few days I located an Ernesto Alaniz, Sr. in Corpus Christi, Texas. It took me a day to track down and find the right phone number.

When I called, a soft-spoken voice answered, "Hello."

"May I talk to Mr. Alaniz?"

"I am he."

I told him I was a captain for the sheriff's office in Flint, Michigan, and I wanted to talk to him about his family. After a few seconds of hesitation he agreed. "Is your first name Ernesto?"

"Yes."

"Is your full name Ernesto Alaniz, Sr.?"

"Yes."

Bam, I got him!

"Sir, your sons have been trying to reach you and would like to talk to you."

Silence.

After a few seconds, I repeated my words.

"Who are you again and why are you calling me?" he asked.

By this time I was getting short tempered because of his obvious hesitation. Then I thought maybe he has a new woman in his life and she doesn't know he has kids from another woman and he never told her. Now he gets this call and she's right next to him. This could be a major obstacle. I repeated my name and purpose.

"Sir, your sons have been trying to reach you and would like to talk to you."

Ernesto Sr. responded in a tense voice. "I don't know who you are or why you are calling, but my sons are sitting right here next to me."

No way, I got this guy and he knows it. "Sir, how old are your sons?"

"They are 12 and 14," he yelled over the phone.

Abort! Abort! I apologized profusely. I found the wrong Ernesto Alaniz, Sr.

How was I to know that the last name of Alaniz in Corpus Christi is as common as Smith in America, Patel in India, or Yoder in Pennsylvania? There were hundreds of them. I needed to dive deeper.

I called the original Ernesto back and demanded more information, no matter how insignificant. I told him I hit a dead end and needed to narrow my search. He called back shortly and stated he had an address from an envelope his mother had given him years back. I wrote down the address, cross-referenced it, and found another Ernesto Alaniz, Sr. But there was no phone number. That didn't stop me. I decided to solicit the services of the Corpus Christi Police Department. All I needed was for them to drop off a business card with my direct number written on the back at the address. They agreed and sent a car. Then it became a waiting game to see if Mr. Alaniz would call.

The day came and went. Thursday came, then Friday, but still no call. On Monday morning, I went to my office and saw a dozen messages on my voicemail. As I listened, I heard the quiet voice of a lady with a distinct Latino accent clearly desperate to talk with me. This was a great sign. Her name was Mrs. Anna Moreno. Though unsure of the connection, I knew it was a breakthrough.

I called Anna and introduced myself, then quickly got to the point. "Mrs. Moreno, I'm trying to reach Ernesto Alaniz, Sr. Do you know him?"

"I do," she said softly.

I gave her more details of the family, which she confirmed, then my heart sank. They had received the card left by the officers on Friday, but the number to call on the back was written incorrectly by the officer. It was off by one digit! They had tried to find me for days but had the wrong number. By God's design, Mrs. Moreno told me she Googled my name to make sure I wasn't some nut-job and to find a correct number. Ironically, it turned out she was on a hunt for me while I was on a hunt for them.

"Mrs. Moreno, is your husband there?"

"Yes, he is. I will put him on the phone."

I heard the shuffling of people and the sound of the phone being transferred from one to another, and then in a stronger Latino accent I heard, "Hello."

"Mr. Alaniz, my name is Captain Chris Swanson. Do you have sons named Ernesto and Antonio?" The silence was deafening. "Sir, did you ever live on the east side of Flint, Michigan?"

More silence, then, "Yes." His voice was thick with emotion.

"Sir, did you leave your family when Ernesto was a child?"

"Yes."

Yahtzee!

"Mr. Alaniz, your boys want to see you again," I said.

If falling tears had sound, I would have heard them crashing to the floor.

Once the initial shock had passed, he begged me to talk to his sons. This was the day long awaited. I promised Mr. Alaniz I would contact his sons and let them know I had found him, and it would be up to them to rekindle the flame. Leaving them with all my correct information, Mr. Alaniz thanked me 10,000 times before we ended our conversation. I asked for Anna to come back to the phone since Sr. was an emotional mess. There were no more questions. She wished me well in a soft voice and I hung up.

God wanted this family to be reunited.

My next phone call was to Ernesto. At the first attempt there was no answer, so I left a voicemail. Unbeknownst to me, he was out of town on vacation with his family. But within an hour he returned my call.

"My brother," he greeted me.

I didn't waste time. "Dude, I found your dad and he wants to talk to you."

Silence. This was becoming a common practice.

"Are you serious, brother?"

"Yes, 100 percent. I talked to him this morning and he wants to talk to you and Antonio."

I'll never know the pain, the suffering, or the loneliness that Ernesto and his brother endured all those years through missed birthdays, fatherless summer days, or the overwhelming sense of abandonment. What I do know is the joy and victory I felt the day two little boys living in grown-up bodies were reunited with their father.

For years, the boys dreamed that if they were to ever find their father, they would make it a celebration and a moment never to forget.

And that's *exactly* what they did.

Later that week, Ernesto and Antonio met for a world-class steak dinner, exchanged memories, and then set a time to call their dad.

I am honored to report ever since that first conversation, they have talked every week, traveled to Texas for family reunions Tex-Mex style, and celebrated holidays together. Once a broken family never thought to be reunited, they *were* restored because of the courage to search *one more time.*

The next summer I had the privilege of going to one of their family reunions in Michigan and meeting the real Ernesto Sr. I must admit it was surreal to see it all come together and witness it live. As I was about to leave,

Ernesto Jr. stopped me and asked to take a family picture. Ernesto Jr., Antonio, Ernesto Alaniz Sr. and me, the gringo in the middle.

In preparing to write this chapter, I called Ernesto Jr. with a final question. "Ernie, considering what you and Antonio went through all those years, what is the one lesson you pray everybody learns from your experience as an abandoned child?"

Ernesto paused a moment. "Swanson, I want people to know that hope can always be restored. I believe it to be true because it happened to me. Don't lose hope."

Enough said.

_____

Impact Theme:

Don't lose hope.

Action Steps:

1. Resolve to follow through on something you've been hesitating about, something you've been putting off.

2. Trust others and reach out for help. You'll never know what they can do for you if you just ask.

3. Never give up. Ever.

18

Two Bodies, But Really Only One

Coming into the field, I knew I'd see death. In my seventh year on the job, I was assigned to the detective bureau. The sheriff sent his detectives to medical examiner investigator school. The training was intense and long. I eventually tested and became a licensed medical examiner investigator (MEI) for the State of Michigan. Whenever someone dies who was not enrolled in hospice or admitted to the hospital, an MEI is assigned to investigate both the scene and the body to determine whether or not there was a need for an autopsy. If the death is ruled "natural," the body is released directly to the funeral home for preparations. If the death was ruled suspicious or criminal in nature, the body is taken to the morgue and scheduled for an autopsy. Those deaths include:

- Homicides

- Suicides
- Traffic Accidents
- Fatal Burns
- All deaths under 18
- Other deaths with suspicious circumstances

I bet you didn't know that when you die, your body becomes the property of the state in which you live. Not until the medical examiner releases their hold on your body are you able to be transported to a funeral home. Give your soul to the Lord, but your dead body belongs to the government.

I was the on-call MEI. It was late and I was fast asleep at home when I received a call from dispatch around 2:00 a.m. There had been a motorcycle accident at I-475 and Robert T. Longway in Flint. I'm not always alert answering the phone that early in the morning. "Hello?" I said groggily.

"Cap, I've got a bad one for you." Now, when your dispatcher is telling you they have a "bad one," you *know* it's gonna be bad.

My standard middle-of -the-night procedure is to call back in two minutes. All I need is 120 seconds to wake up. I get out of bed and start walking around so I can speak in clear and intelligent sentences. Then I call back, which I did.

"Cap, it's a motorcycle accident but there are two scenes."

By this time I was awake but didn't understand what the dispatcher was saying. "What do you mean two scenes?"

 "Well, he is cut in half and he's on both sides of the highway."

Seriously? This was not going to be pretty. When you realize you're about to see things you don't normally see, it takes a bit to wrap your head around what to expect.

On the way there, my curiosity ran wild. *How does a guy get cut in two?* But once I got to the scene and started my investigation, I figured it out. Here's how:

The last person to see the motorcyclist alive was a driver coming home on the outside lane when the motorcyclist flew past her at over 100 mph! Just ahead, the expressway made a curve to the right, which he couldn't negotiate. At that speed (almost 200 feet per second), it's almost impossible to make a split-second decision. It's all chance, and he took too much of it. His motorcycle rode up the inside wall and went airborne. While in the air, he went one way and his bike went another. As his body was free spinning, a light pole that lit the roadway between the northbound and southbound lanes stopped him mid-flight. That, my friend, cut him in two.

As I walked the scene, I could see different body parts scattered about. On the northbound side was a kidney. On the southbound side was the other kidney. The man's liver rested on the center line, and his stomach between that and the fast lane marker. The rest of his parts were distributed along the roadway. While the top and bottom half of his body looked somewhat "normal," they were 50 feet from each other.

After hours of investigating, we gathered him up, put him in body bags—yes in bags—and sent him to the morgue. I thought, *Why would anyone risk their life by going so fast at night around a corner, not knowing what is to come?*

The answer is shockingly simple: We all do stupid stuff. Consequences come after every decision.

There is no question the victim was conscious as he flew through the air. But it was too late.

_____

Impact Theme:
Recognize the consequences before you do something you know is dangerous or reckless.

Action Steps:

1. Know the pros and cons before making a decision.

2. Know your decisions will always impact other people.

3. If you're stupid, you have only one person to blame.

19

Gentlemen, What You Just Witnessed Was a Miracle.

As a medical examiner investigator, I was called to investigate a death in Grand Blanc Township from the night before.

Mr. Roy McFadden and his wife had enjoyed a great day together. She had been battling cancer for some time but wasn't expected to die anytime soon. Later that evening, she wasn't feeling well and told her husband she was going to go upstairs to lie down.

Before Roy went to bed, he went to check her and found her sleeping peacefully in their master bedroom. Deciding not to disturb her, he went to sleep in the spare bedroom. Around 4:30 a.m. he awoke to go the restroom. On the way he looked into the room and saw she hadn't moved. Running to her bedside, he realized his beautiful wife had breathed her last breath during the night. She was lifeless and cold to the touch. He ran downstairs in a panic and called 911. The police and ambulance arrived soon after, but there was nothing anyone could do. She was already gone.

When I got the call as the on-call MEI it was around 6:15 a.m., I remember it being a bright, hot June morning. When I arrived, the Grand Blanc Township officers were on scene but the ambulance had already left once the EMI confirmed she was dead. I was now in medical examiner mode.

When I talked to Roy, he told me the story as I have written it. Understandably, he was upset and sobbing. I told him I needed to go upstairs to his wife and complete additional investigation. This includes taking photos of the body, the scene, and measurements from both. Once the process was complete, I could send his wife to the desired funeral home for his preparation. I make a point to explain to the grieving families what happens next. I keep it short and sweet.

I went upstairs to take my scene photos and measurements. I confirmed there was nothing suspicious about the death. As I returned downstairs, I watched Roy coming out of the back bathroom. He was clearly upset, knowing what had happened but unable to grasp the reality of her being gone. His son, Patrick, had just arrived.

In an attempt to comfort Roy, I told him that I had been to many scenes where the families of the deceased had no hope. They didn't have faith in Christ, and emptiness filled their hearts and minds. They were lost. This, however, was not that scene. I could tell this family had hope, and a lot of it. There was no question Roy loved her and his deceased wife loved her family. I told him that his wife was no longer in pain and, as a believer, she was in heaven with Jesus. Roy took it all in. *He's going to be alright,* I thought. Just then Roy stiffened up, gasped a long breath, and dropped dead in cardiac arrest right before me.

"Dad!" Patrick screamed.

It was a scene out of the hundreds of CPR classes I've done. As soon as Roy dropped to the floor, I ripped open his shirt and started chest compressions. I hollered for the township officers to grab the automatic external defibrillator (AED) from their patrol car. I continued doing compressions and thought, *This is going to be a great story.*

His son could only watch what was going on. The officers ran back with their AED. As soon as I slapped the pads on his chest, per protocol, it was ready to shock and it shocked him good. No change. More compressions, then another shock was readied. It had been almost eight minutes when the second shock was delivered. Roy's eyes popped open! He started looking around. I checked the pulse in his carotid artery. I checked the pulse in his radial artery. Then I said out loud, "Gentleman, what you just witnessed here was a miracle."

A few minutes later, Roy started talking. "What happened? What happened?"

Through tears, his son said, "Dad, you just died and now you're back." As Patrick cried, it dawned on me that his mom was dead upstairs and his dad just came back to life. Now that's an eventful morning!

The ambulance returned, and Roy was taken to Genesys Hospital. Two days later, he walked out of the hospital, fully recovered. Almost a month after the funeral for his wife, I was able to connect with Patrick. I had known him from the past. He's a good dude.

"Hey, Patrick, how's your dad?" I asked.

He explained things had settled after the funeral, but the adjustment was hard.

Then I asked another question that I believe everybody wants to ask. "What's the last thing your dad remembers?"

Who doesn't want to know that, right? Did he see the light or smell smoke?

Patrick told me he asked his dad the same thing. He told him he didn't remember most of what had happened before the cardiac arrest except talking to me. The whole room grew quiet, then everything went dark. Nothing more.

Then I added a monster follow-up question: "Dude, what's the first thing he remembered?"

He said it was like he was being awakened from a deep sleep unable to focus his eyes, yet hearing people around him. The first words he heard were, "Gentleman, what you just witnessed here was a miracle."

That's awesome! Those were my words! How cool is that?

Roy McFadden is my hero!

A true miracle of second chances and second chances are beautiful.

Roy is alive today and I am honored to have played a role.

_____

Impact Theme:
Second chances come in all forms and often when you least expect them.

Action Steps:
1. Be careful not to judge by what you see on the surface.
2. Always look to give others a second chance.
3. Sometimes you are the receiver, sometimes you are the giver. Appreciate them both.

20

The Greatest Family I've Ever Met

I met an incredible family on Sunday, February 21, 2016. Prior to this day, we had never crossed paths. They lived just down the road from me: Mom and Dad and their four beautiful kids, ages eleven, nine, seven and two. When I was called to their house, the first one I met was the dad; he was in the basement. Turns out he was the spiritual leader of the family. Under his watch, the family served many people through their local church. They had just returned from family movie night. Once Dad and I met, I then met the nine-year-old boy who was dressed to play like any other boy would dress on a Saturday morning. Next, the seven-year-old girl had just stepped out of the shower and was getting ready herself. As I moved to the upstairs, the oldest boy was in his room, reading a book in his bunk bed. Finally, Mom and her youngest were in the nursery. She had just fed him breakfast, a fresh-baked cinnamon roll, and was getting him ready for a mid-morning nap. I really wanted to talk to them and get to know them better.

But that was impossible.

They were all dead.

Just before receiving the call, I had been in my basement recording a video for my "Ask the Ironman" show when Jamie came into the studio with a concerned look on her face. She told me she had just received a call from my captain, Casey Tafoya, to advise there was a home right around the corner where six people were found dead inside, most likely from carbon monoxide poisoning. Officers and firefighters had just arrived on scene and were already reporting on the horrific scene. It would be my job to find out what had happened and how.

I quickly changed my clothes, then raced to the location. A few minutes later, I pulled into the driveway and braced for impact. The house was wrapped in crime scene tape. As I headed to the front door, I could smell the toxic gas. Carbon monoxide itself is odorless and colorless, but in exhaust form you never forget the smell. Like burned bodies, you never forget.

This was going to be a long night.

Officers scurried around, knowing I would be the lead of a long-term investigation. I gathered my two detectives, who were already on the scene, as well as the two responding officers. I wanted to talk to each one of them individually to find out what exactly they had seen when they first arrived. That's one of the most effective things a police investigator can do at a crime scene—get the facts, starting from the beginning.

After the fire department cleared the toxic air from the house using mega fans, we entered the crime scene and began our process. I have seen a lot of dead bodies, but never six at the same time and never an entire family wiped out at once. This poor family never knew what had hit them as they died in their steps throughout the house. Here is their story.

On the Friday two days before the family was found, the power had been knocked out by a vicious storm. The father had gone to Home Depot around 10:00 p.m. that night to get a cord and sockets in order to hook up his propane generator, which he kept in his basement. Once he connected the power cord to the electric panel box, he fired up the generator and power to the house was restored. He must have thought that because he was burning propane, the fumes were not toxic.

That was a fatal mistake.

As fumes filled the nighttime air, carbon monoxide in the basement increased dramatically. In the morning, he must have gone to the basement to check the generator. As he opened the door, toxic fumes filled the house, displacing all oxygen. Without oxygen, it takes less than eight seconds for a person to be asphyxiated and pass out. That's why this poor family was scattered throughout the house with no sign of attempted escape. They had literally died in their tracks.

We already had utility experts, propane experts, generator experts, electrical experts, and furnace experts on scene to confirm what had happened that weekend was not a failure of machinery or failure of utilities, but the result of a devastating decision.

It was obvious there was no premeditation or suspicion on anyone's part. It was just a very sad accident.

If this were not difficult enough, the time I had to meet the surviving family didn't exactly excite me. However, they turned out to be some amazing people whom I love to this day.

As I walked toward the hill, I was not alone. Two of my dearest friends were shoulder-to-shoulder with me: Lieutenant Bill Lanning, who also lived right around the corner, and my Ironman partner, Captain Casey Tafoya. We could see the family huddled together. Our steps were heavy. The landscape closed in faster than I wanted. Next thing I knew, I was face-to-face with Mom,

Dad, Grandpa and Grandma, sister, sister- in-law, and the closest of friends. Their eyes were red from tears.

I took a deep breath. "I am so sorry for your loss. My name is Chris Swanson, the undersheriff, and I am here to answer any questions you have and try to give as much comfort as I possibly can."

I expected screams, belly sobs, or some other expression. Instead I heard Laura, the deceased father's mom. "Chris, it's you!"

What? How do they know me?

Laura moved forward and hugged me, explaining they had just heard me preach just a few months ago at the River church. In fact, she told me the verse I used was taped to their bathroom mirror. I Timothy 6:6 *But Godliness with Contentment is Great Gain!*

Thank you, Jesus! They were my people. Because of this connection, I was able to work through the scene without nearly as much pain.

Listen to me. When you have to deal with tragedy, there are two ways people respond: with hope because of Jesus or without hope because they are lost. When you are forced to deal with people who are hopeless, it's so hard to comfort them because it is so final. They can't wrap their head around the finality of death. With Jesus in their lives, people are sad but know they will be reunited again with their loved ones. Friend, if you have never accepted Jesus in your life, I implore you to do so today. Not tomorrow. Death has no boundaries.

The night weighed heavy on all the investigators and responders. For hours we methodically moved room by room, taking photos, measuring, and collecting evidence with one goal in mind—to find out what happened.

Once the scene was processed, it was time to remove the family and transport them to the morgue for examination by the pathologist. As we waited for the transport service to arrive, Phil, the deceased father's father, asked if he could go inside and pray. I quickly led him as far as I could, which was just inside the garage entry in the laundry room. He could see down the hall. It was all too familiar, since he was the one who booted the door, found his family, and called 911. When we stopped, I could feel the heaviness in his heart and felt so bad for him. He could see, smell, and feel the loss. Instantly, we broke out in prayer, begging the Lord for comfort and guidance. Phil needed to know his Lord will never leave him nor forsake him.

I can't even tell you what words I muttered in prayer. What do you say in these circumstances? But our prayer time was a precious moment, one that we still talk about today. What seemed like an hour was over quickly, and I escorted Phil back to his wife, Laura, and went about our business.

The body removal service arrived in three dark mini-vans around 8:00 p.m. I was surprised how fast they responded only to find out they had been staged around the corner, knowing that expediting the removal would be on everybody's short list. They were gracious. We placed each precious victim in the sterile white bags, then tagged and sealed each bag. Each one was more difficult than the one prior, and I did all I could to hold back my rage and tears.

The six bags were loaded into the transport vans.

Slam!

The door closed.

More reality.

As the vans drove away, I felt as though part of the living went with them. It was now time for us to secure and clear the scene. My detectives and I conducted a final walk through to close all doors and windows that were opened for ventilation. I purposely chose to clear the upstairs where three of the victims were found.

At the top of the stairs and to my left was the oldest boy's bedroom, a bathroom in the middle, and another bedroom to my right decked out in pink. The baby's nursery was to my far right. I stopped in the hallway and prayed. I prayed for the family. I prayed for strength and understanding. I prayed for that day to be used in a way that makes me a better man; that the day would not be seen as just another tragedy, but somehow, some way, good would come. Amen. I then headed back downstairs and out through the garage. As we all filed out, I felt like none of us really wanted to leave, but did not want to be there either. I hit the outside garage door opener and the big white door slowly lowered. The images of a kid's bike with training wheels, the backyard grill, a lawnmower, and basketballs faded into the darkness.

The last thing was to remove the massive amounts of crime scene tape from the perimeter. Finally, the scene was secured. Time to leave.

My drive home was silent, but my mind was screaming. I pulled into my driveway, opened my garage door and pulled into a home of peace, family, and love. Why is life so unfair to some and not others? Why do some lose everything and others nothing? I'll never know. Shortly thereafter, I showered, then slipped into a deep sleep, only to wake up and do it all over again.

Since that day, this family has been able to share the Gospel of Jesus Christ to thousands of lost souls across the globe. They started the "Q Project," which is committed to providing free carbon monoxide detectors to everyone who needs them throughout the United States. They are taking a horrific situation and making lifetime impact.

I love this family and they love me. They are truly the Greatest Family I Ever Met!

_____

Impact Theme:

Good can come out of bad, if you look for it. I met incredible people that night, starting with the man's father, Mr. Phil Quazzarano. He showed me what a man of strength is supposed to look like under the worst conditions. As I did my job, he held the remaining family together and was their rock. To this day, Phil and I are brothers in Christ.

Action Steps:

1. Realize that what you are doing always involves other people.
2. Don't just rely on your own judgment; ask others. Be informed.
3. Appreciate the times you were protected from your stupidity. Most of us can think of times when we were ignorant or careless and somehow got away with it. Be thankful, but also be more careful.

Conclusion

Finish with your PhD

Here's a truth about life: Bad things will happen to both the just and the unjust. But so will incredible things! I told these stories with the purpose of challenging you to learn every day, to appreciate the gifts and blessings you wake up to, and to encourage you to look forward to the amazing things that are going on around you. Take time for the people who love you. Recognize the value of your skills and education. Take advantage of your athletic ability, even if that means going for a walk around the block. Anything and everything that is important to you needs to be valued, cared for, and remembered. You never know when something—or someone—will be taken away.

I am just like you; I sometimes start the day with an attitude. But when I wake up that way, it doesn't take me long before I get to work to see what real pain is. What real poverty looks like. What hunger does to people.

It's been said many times: When you compare your pile of problems to the pile of problems of the one next to you, you'll gladly take yours.

In closing, I want you to commit to three things for the rest of your life:

1. Live with PASSION in all you do.
2. Create a HUNGER to do more, be more, and give more.
3. Become so DISCIPLINED in your life that every day you work your guts out toward your goals and dreams.

If you put this plan into action and commit to it, when the day comes for a story to be told about you, others will celebrate the way you lived, and you will have earned your PhD in life: PASSION – HUNGER – DISCIPLINE.

Don't live your life in vain. Live to make a difference, and make a difference in someone's life—starting today!

Until next time ...

Chris

About the Author

Christopher Swanson is a career police officer with experiences spanning more than two decades. He has served in a variety of positions, including corrections, patrol, narcotics, criminal investigation, death investigation, and command operations. Some of his most notable assignments have been part of the executive protection for President George W. Bush and Barack Obama and Vice Presidents Gore, Chaney, and Biden.

Christopher commands the police honor guard, which has performed over 100 ceremonies across the state. He currently holds the rank of undersheriff in the Office of Sheriff, a 252-member agency located within Flint, Michigan, one of the most dangerous cities in the nation. He augments his police experience as a licensed paramedic and certified medical examiner investigator. This training has led him to witness some of the most heinous crimes and acts of violence one can imagine, including homicides, suicides, felonies, fatalities, and drug overdoses. He shares these experiences with audiences across the country to make a positive impact in their lives, using lessons from the living and the dead.

Chris is also the best-selling author of *Tinman to Ironman*, a sought-after speaker, and he holds both a master's degree in public administration and a bachelor's degree from the University of Michigan, along with numerous national and state certifications.

As an athlete, he is a four-time IRONMAN finisher and a lifelong bodybuilder. You can learn more about Chris at www.swansonleadership.com.